THEN A STORM

By

FERRIS E. JONES

ISBN: 978-93-6354-371-3

First Edition: 2025
Rs. 200/-

Cyberwit.net
HIG 45 Kaushambi Kunj, Kalindipuram
Allahabad - 211011 (U.P.) India
http://www.cyberwit.net
Tel: +(91) 9415091004
E-mail: info@cyberwit.net

Printed at Repro India Limited.

This book is dedicated to
my best friend Johnny.
(Kurt Johnson)

Contents

The End

What I witnessed
at his end,
will never go away.
It will remain
like your wedding day,
or the birth
of your first child.
Appearing
out of nowhere,
because of a voice,
song, or smell.
It will ponder
and destroy
my resting before bed,
for the rest of my life.
What did he see?
What was he trying to say?

A reclining chair
would be where
he took his last breath.
He had not spoken
or moved on his own
for days now,
so, the end
was coming soon.
And me,
not more than
four feet away.

I was copying
and stapling
some papers
that were signed
to protect him.
He stood up
on his own,
looked at me
with total shock,
and tried to speak.
All that came out
was some sort
of groan.
He fell back
into his seat
and smiled.
He was gone.
What did he see?
What was he trying to say?

My Ears

The truth was not loud,
just calm, behind my ears.
Photos kept quiet
the misplaced grace
of a whispered lie.

I have so many names,
all wrapped in ink.
Scattered shadows
have no more blood
to give. Obscure eyes
continue to come searching.

Flawed are the stories
told of undoing. Yet
the thread of false prophecy
cannot see its reflection.
I replace the missing words
with my woven being.

Killer

The little boy
didn't wake up
intending
to kill anybody
that morning,
but he did.
They ruled it
a suicide
since the gun
was next to him.

His wife
put it there.
She heard the shot
and saw the boy. He
went to hide
in the treehouse.
She called the cops
and said the old man
was an alcoholic, he
couldn't get over
the war.

It made sense, he
put Jack Daniels
in his coffee
that morning.
She knew
what he did. The boy

new what he did.
God knew
what he did.

From the treehouse
the boy watched
the body
being removed.
Watched
as the police
believe
every word.
Watched as his
little sister
smiled
back at him.
She knew
where he was.
She knew what
her brother
had done,
and why
he had done it.

Seediest

It did not matter
where my family lived.
He would always find
the seediest area of town
and make it his own.
It would be somewhat of a strip,
where he could go
from bar to bar,
and get food on occasion.
He would make sure
everybody knew him,
and everybody feared him.
Violence was always
part of how he lived.
When I was a kid,
all I would have to do
was ride my bike to the strip,
walk in and ask for my father.
Everybody knew
what bar he was in.
That is where I would find him
when I needed something to eat.
After a coke and some beef jerky,
I could convince him
to hand over a little cash,
then it was a feast
for me and my little sister.
Fast food for a hungry kid
is a feast.

Not much changed as
I grew older except the family
was no longer together,
and my father found a new state,
and a new strip to rule over.
One weekend around the time
I was attending a community college,
me and my best friend Johnny
decided to get some beer
and go fishing.
It just so happened
that to get to our fishing spot
we had to drive right through
the middle of the strip.
My guess now is that place became
our fishing spot because
someone on the strip told
my father about it.
As we were driving,
I noticed my father's car
at a little mom and pop Diner.
This is where the drunks
would go hang out and eat
until the bars reopened
in a couple of hours.
You could not miss my father's car,
It was the ugliest, rusted out
Ford Pinto you had ever seen.
The funny part about it was
it looked good when
my mother bought it new.

The first thing we noticed
when we pulled into the parking lot

was the burned-out car.
It looked like someone blew it up,
just like in the movies.
We walked in and then
we saw my father sitting with
some of his drinking friends.
We walk over and sit down,
and I ask him how he is doing.
Of course, he says he is fine,
but nobody is fine
when they are about to start
their third straight day of drinking.
I asked him what happened
to the car outside
and he and his friends
started to look at each other
and laugh.
He says,
"See that ugly prick over there
by himself,
it's his car,
and I thought
the fucker was in it."
Again, they all began to laugh.
It was time for me to leave now.
It finally hit me,
why not more
than a couple of weeks earlier,
he told me to never
go to the strip by myself.
He said certain people will know
I am his son,
and it may not turn out
so well for me.

Delinquent

Vincent was my best friend,
when I was about eight years old.
I remember my father
catching the palm tree on fire
across the street in his yard.
My father had to explain
to Vincent's mother
why he was drunk and
shot a bottle rocket up into her tree.
He of course lied to the police officers
and the fire department.
It was Vincent's yard that became
the centerfield fence.
When all of us neighbor kids
gathered and played baseball,
my yard back by the fence was home plate
and Vincent's yard meant a home run.
First base was the old plumb tree,
second base was the sidewalk,
and third base was whatever car
was in the driveway.
Even as a little kid,
I hit a bunch of home runs.

Vincent's back yard was our fort.
He had a big tree and shade.
I think that house was built before ours.
I would spend the night at his house,
and we would camp out in the backyard.
Things were quite different back in the 1970's.

My father did not really like black
people over at our house,
but even though I was white,
Vincent's mother did not mind at all.
At eight years old black or white
never even crossed our minds.
I hear he is a minister now.
I can see that.
He came from a good family.
His father had died in Vietnam,
while my father lived and returned,
with a chip on his shoulder.
Vincent's mother worked extremely hard,
he was not an only child,
but he was the youngest.
Their family was no different
than any other family, and I
did not let other kids say anything different.
My father made me be a bully at times.

Fried bologna was
our camping food of choice.
He had this little hot plate,
and we would run an extension cord
into the house. But catsup on bologna,
not for me. I always had mustard.
His house was a safe place for me.
Sometime when I was about
nine or ten years old, and Vincent
and his family had moved away,
I was still searching for that safe place.
Being a bit of a delinquent,
some kids and I went to 7-11
and stole a couple of bottles of wine.

I got drunk and passed out
in the broken-down car
they had in their driveway.
Their mother was supposed to be
my babysitter
while my parents were out.
She was never a babysitter,
just another drunk loser
who could not take care
of her own kids.
After waking up in the car scared
and not really understanding
what happened or why
I was where I was.
I walked down the street
to Vincent's house.
My best guess was it was about midnight.
I began crying as I knocked on the door.
The tears faded away immediately
when a white women stood there
looking at me.
At the time I did not understand why
she looked the way she did,
but she scared me.
After telling me she had never
heard of Vincent,
her sister came to the door.
I was interrupting a party.
The smell of weed, loud music
and people were everywhere.
The nice, obviously younger sister
took me into the kitchen,
and called my mother to get me.
My mother always came to get me.

The Intertwined Falcon

(1)
Things are different
when you live in a small town.
Those who live in a city
cannot even imagine how
intertwined people's lives get.
One night at the local tavern,
where everyone knows your business,
I met a girl named Amy.
(Crazy Bitch)
Come to find out her father
who was the district attorney
back in the day
"Dad, I heard you used to be friends
with a guy named Johnny Black."
"Yeah why."
The chick I brought home the other night
said she is his daughter."
"Was it TJ or Amy."
"Amy." Good because that other bitch is ugly."
"Johnny Black was a good guy."
I whooped up on this one guy
down in Tonopah one time
when you were little,
and it was him that told the judge
it could not have been me because
I was with him.
He saved my ass boy."
(Of course he did)

(2)
After Amy and I had a lot of drinks,
which I paid for,
we went back to my mobile home.
Yes, mobile home.
Then someone started knocking at the door.
I said, "who is it?"
"I need to talk to Amy."
"Amy isn't here dude, go home."
"I know she's in there."
Then of course Amy had to say something,
"Go away Julian and mind your own business."
I asked Amy who that guy was,
and she said it was her old boyfriend.
He did not get the memo and was a little upset
someone was taking his girlfriend home.
I opened the door and there stood
a muscle-bound Hispanic guy.
"Dude, what do you want?"
"I want to talk to Amy."
"Well, she doesn't want to talk to you."
As he is reaching behind him and pulling
out an extraordinarily long knife, he says,
"You are going to get her right now."
Before saying anything, I reach over
to the kitchen table,
which is only two feet away,
because I live in a mobile home,
and grabbed my gun
and point it at his face.
"Get the fuck out of here
before I put a bullet in your head."
(Another dumbass who has no idea)

Realizing he lost this round he leaves.
Not without saying something
to the effect that he will get me later.
Which of course he never did
because he was a punk bitch.

(3)
A few months later I met another girl
at the same local tavern.
I did not take her home or anything,
just a little make out session in the ally.
Come to find out shortly after
I met this young lady,
Julian breaks into her apartment,
locks her child in the closet
and then rapes her repeatedly for twelve hours.
(Scumbag)
This is when I realize
it would have been much better
for everyone if I just shot him
when I had the chance
and claimed self-defense.
I mean he was standing on my porch
with a knife in his hand.
I could not get over this terrible thing
happening to such a nice person.
Obviously, this was exceedingly difficult for her,
and she had to move out of her appointment.
There could be no way anybody
could continue to live in the same place
that something so horrible happened.
(I had no idea what was coming)
She moved out of town to get

this part of her life behind her.
Again, months go by,
and I lead my otherwise boring life.
I sell my mobile home,
then I buy another one,
just to rent them out for extra income.
I moved into an apartment
which seemed nice.
It had a little yard outside,
and an extra bedroom I turned into a gym.

(4)
Out of nowhere, I got a letter
calling me to jury duty.
I had never been on a jury before,
so, I was excited.
As with any small town,
when I arrived, I knew everyone
else who received a letter,
then the gossip started.
(This guy is going to be guilty)
In a matter of about 15 minutes
of listening to everyone discuss
the fact that they thought we were all there
because it was the trail for Julian,
I was freaked out.
People already knew specific details
of how Julian had raped that young woman.
They discussed the address and location
of the apartment,
what apartment number it was,
and how he got in.
That is when I realized

that it was my new apartment.
My jacket is hanging in the closet
where he locked the young child.
My bed is now in the same place
her bed was in when he raped her
for twelve hours.
(I wanted to cry)
It broke my heart,
why did I not just kill that guy
when I had the chance.
Then they bring us all into a room
and ask us if anybody present
knows the defendant
and cannot be impartial.
I raised my hand and was dismissed,
feeling as if what had happened
to that young girl was my fault.
Why didn't I just shoot him?
I could have lived with that
much better than the young women and her child
having to live with fear and terror
that will never go away.
(This shit lasts forever)
Be careful,
and select your choices well,
we have no idea how our lives
are intertwined.
Even though Julian was sentenced to life in prison,
and has since died in that very prison,
I feel a sense of guilt every day.
I hope that young lady
and her child are doing well.
I cannot even remember her name.
(What a dick I have become)

Beyond the Day and Night

Beyond the day and night
falls a silent path.
Whispers of walls
lead the way.
The rhythm of a gate
can be felt.

Each breath, a beat
towards the light.
Logic, clarity
forms a melody.
Truth gets warmed
by the movement.

The abyss collides
in words.
Currents, emotions
are endless.
Flash and rage
sit still.

A universe, a journey
vast and spun.
With endless grace
and simplicity.
It ends with soft, kind
intertwined joys.

The Gift

No skies, open limits,
the gift to you.
The pure glide
of every step
parts clouds
with the heart
of this
sacred grace.

My End

Rivers flow, a world
walked by me.
Mountains touched
with visions from me.
Skies journey unbound
the path for me.
The prize that awaits
is our end.
The prize that awaits
is our friend.

Today and Tonight

Goodbye birds,
glowing and clear.
The hue of evening
is earlier this year.

Blooms cry off,
sunflowers turn.
Sunsets, are few,
while new fires burn.

Swallowed

What is the point
I prayed.
The evidence shows
upon death
the world ends.
All your goods
are swallowed
and allowed
to decay.

It's a formula,
a simple one of
remembrance
and death.
Not a man
on the moon,
Does the flag
wave or not
in the wind?

Coca Cola

No more ice cream
or Coca Cola.
The TV repair man
is dead.
The Maytag guy
rests next to
the Charmin guy.
Where's the Beef?
It's in stocks
and bonds.
Laughing at
your eight dollars
cup of coffee.

The Right and Left Hand of God

Fighting for your life
brings with it
a good death.
How many baby daddies
that bitch have,
anyway?

Food and love
provided, paves
for the future.
When was the last time
she held a job,
not just you?

The right words are simple,
the wrong words can
bring tag along death.
When did she love
you last,
or cast,
your eye?

Solitude

Turmoil, rush, and roar,
the quiet of life dies.
No tranquil space for
secrets to hide.
I ask for nothing,
time, be on my side.

No judgements to craft,
for wandering space.
It's the gem in time
that soars in desire
collecting one's fate.

There's depth is sound,
pounding the stillness dead.
Unburdened silence leaks
Into a stillness,
perfect for my head.

Poetry and Art

In the moment of the flash,
will the memories cease?
The waters?
Will the cardinals change,
a new era of wishes
and past delights,
later, to be forgotten?

Washing His Clothes

(1)

"Let me tell you Eddie,
I am the most chicken shit son of a bitch
that ever lived."
That is how my father, on his death bed began the conversation.
It was not much of a surprise to me to hear him say that.
I had seen him in action.
It did not matter if it was a pool cue, ashtray, or beer bottle,
he was going to use whatever he needed
to make sure he won that fight.
The bigger they were,
the more violent he became.
I remember him telling me when I was a kid,
"Boy, you have the heart, and you have the balls,
but you are just too light in the ass
to be messing with the big boys."
The funny thing was, he was only five foot nine.
The key for him was to, "never get hurt."
By that he meant not getting yourself in a situation
where you can no longer defend yourself.
This coming from a man who was shot,
stabbed, and beaten so badly
his kidneys did not function.
This was something I always took to heart.
It was also the reason he called himself
the most chicken shit son of a bitch in the world.
He always landed the first blow.
The fight was always on his terms.

He fought in bars and the streets
well into his fifties.

(2)

In the sixty years of my life,
it took my father all of them
before he sat me down and explained
those stories I grew up hearing.
At 79 years old and having been
smoking four packs of cigarettes
a day for 65 years,
he was dying of lung cancer,
and not from cigarettes.
He was exposed to asbestos
during the Vietnam war and
was slowly dying of Mesothelioma.
He had spent six years in the navy
aboard the aircraft carrier USS Ticonderoga.
He always claimed he was
the most decorated Vietnam vet in the state.
I could never confirm that,
but to this day
I still remember wearing his medals
when I was a little boy.
When he passed away and I received his DD214
from the government to provide to the cemetery.
He had an extensive list of honors.
I still do not know what they all meant.
I do know after keeping the secret for 25 years
that the Ticonderoga lost a nuclear warhead
off the south China sea and that he was there.
I had asked him about it

when it finally hit the news and he said,
"I was standing right there, I could see his eyes
and watched him go right over the side."
Later I read my father was telling the truth.
Other witnesses stated the pilot was not wearing
his helmet as the plane slowly went overboard.
The pilot's body was never recovered,
only the helmet,
which he was not wearing.

(3)

So, as my father sits on his recliner,
slowly dying he continues
with his long confession.
I will call it that,
but that is not what it really was.
It was more of just letting me know
who he really was,
in case I had any misconceptions.
He wanted me to know that he was not
at all sorry for the things he had done.
He just wanted me to know his reasons
for doing them.
He genuinely believes, the people
he hurt had it coming. And in most cases,
I believe he was right.
"I never killed anybody,
I know people think I did,
but I didn't," he said.
"I tried to kill Robert,
and I thought I did,
but the prick lived.

" I asked, "Did you shoot him or what?"
"No, I beat the son of a bitch to death,
at least I tried to."
The reason I asked if he had shot him,
was due to a memory I had a kid.
Now I am not sure if it was a dream
or it was real. In my mind,
as a kid, it was a fact, I was there,
I heard the shot, and the guy
did not come back.
But now my father says he never killed anybody,
so, what am I to believe?
I went to unusual places with my father.
Sometimes it was to work,
but mostly it was to bars,
or to visit his low life friends.
I know now that these were not visits,
and guns or drugs were being
exchanged or discussed.
I knew these people were scumbags.
Even at eight years old,
I knew what drug paraphernalia was,
even if I never heard the term.
I knew what a bunch of drunks
and naked women laying around
on the couches and floors meant
in relation to the previous night's activities.
I also knew how to navigate the bar scene
and who to speak to and who not to speak it.
You notice that quickly
when you spend your summers
shooting pool, eating beef jerky
and watching your father drink all day.

(4)

I have always believed
I was riding in the back seat of the car,
my father was driving,
and one of his friends
was in the passenger seat.
I recall my father driving
up into the hills outside Los Angeles.
This was not uncommon.
I remember being in that area lots of times as a kid.
I remember my father telling me to
duck down in the back seat,
again, not an uncommon thing.
But what I remember most
was my father pulling over
and he and his friend got out of the car.
It seemed like a long time,
but then I heard a gunshot.
These too were not uncommon for me to hear,
so, it was clear to me, that is what I heard.
Then my father came back to the car by himself,
got in and we drove away.
He never said a word about it.
Now on his death bed he says
he never killed anybody,
but he did in fact try to.

(5)
"I beat that man until I could not beat him anymore,
everyone thought I had killed him," he said.
"Why, what did he do?" I spoke.
"He was my best friend Eddie,

and that prick fucked me over."
"Me and a bunch of people went
to Jim Butler days in Tonopah,
you know what that is right?"
"Yeah, I have been there."
"Well, I could not find my old lady anywhere,
and then someone said they saw her and Robert
go into the bar across the street.
When I got there, I could see the back of them,
and they were sitting at the bar
talking with some bikers.
Come to find out,
I overheard them,
Robert was making a deal
on the side without me,
a big deal."
I dragged his ass out the door by his feet
and beat him worse than any man
I had ever beaten before in my life,
I just knew he was dead."
"But he lived right."
"I didn't know that though,
another buddy and me jumped in the car
and drove the two hours back home.
He dropped me off at the bar
and I ordered a drink.
Then acted like I had been there all day."
" I asked, "when did you find out he was alive."
"I was only in the bar for about five minutes
when the cops came in and handcuffed me
and said I was under arrest for murder.
Then, just as those chicken shit bastards
were putting me in the car,

a radio call said he was still alive
and was being flown to the hospital.
Those cops uncuffed me,
let me go, and they never asked me about it again.
Of course, they knew better too."
I had always assumed it was Robert
my father killed in the hills of Los Angeles,
it was not. I asked my father,
"Did you ever see him again?"
"Nope, but I kept looking for him
every time I went back to L.A."

Old Christmas

The snow wraps my soul
on cruel days.
Open to the air,
the cold pain bites
at the toes of moments
that crackle a fleeting voice,
unspoken, silent, echoing,
while it fills
this empty space.

Emily

Her eyes grew deep
with a vast burned struggle.
Revealing a calm whisper
disguised as a river,
flowing strong along
a path of night.
Growing a soul,
unwinding a death,
filling the darkest
sky that lingers.

It Started

It started,
the flashes of my childhood
have come to television.
Cinque lives,
reincarnated on the internet.
He hands out flowers
held in the teeth of
a seven-headed cobra.

Patty Hearst is a star
without talent, they will be
coming for her latest version.
The funds are everywhere,
black, excessive, and boisterous.
The president will be humiliated,
old, and panicked, he will pass.
The country will be divided
on which story to follow.

Hopeful this will not Linger

The fading carries as it
jostles back and forth
between breath and death.
The stories stopped flowing.
The face loses its grip. Strings
unravel the roses' silence. Joy,
deep in hiding
speaks goodbye.
Flight will be soon,
It will come quietly,
and final. I will remain,
stranded, hopeful this
will not linger.

Lunch with Patti Smith

She wandered my apartment.
"I am also a poet," I said.
Her bold voice replied,
"Do you write like Hemingway"?
After untangling the plants
blocking the book titles,
she smiled. The map
of her mind was visible,
and I wanted to be nearby.

"The world may change," she said.
I laughed, "Not within these
walls it won't, ink is a place
of belonging, and mine
never fades." With rhythm,
we walked past the truth. Past
the bookstore downstairs,
around the corner of worn spines,
to settle at a deli.

Rhythm

Whiskey's edge by the sea
Sunburnt skin in waves
Sticks for feet
Hair for days
Laughter for children.

It is golden
The rhythm
Of the moon
In memory of
Not feeling the years.

Toil Not

Is it coming,
Is it time?
The shallow shadow,
is it here?

It is never in a hurry,
until it is.

It is familiar,
I have seen it many times.
It fights and whispers.
when it holds
familiar face.

Toil not,
it is endless.
in its pursuit.

Cruelty

A bruised whispered fear
has no walls.
No dreams of kindness
to survive the day.
Small hands reach
to the sky.
They want to be good
in silence.

What Remains

Dusk is quiet,
the flame hushed.
Muted justice
has become fear.

The cost
is crushing.
Dim nights
have become clear.

Crowds, the truth,
are denied.
Death to rights,
power, and laws.

People, untamed,
cold and beating.
God's only
son withdraws.

Without Business

You cannot bargain
your way in
or out. It is a song,
quiet, no promises,
just gifts, forever.
A garden without
trade, without business.
A connection with
no price tag or payment.
It settles, it dwells
in having you
and only you.

Then a Storm

Its whisper shifts.
Our roots grow weaker
by its fleeting. Caught
in its warning, we fade.
Then grasp at moments
that melts our sky. There
will be a rebirth, a death,
then a storm.

This Coming Dawn

A bruised torn
endless night.
Twirling fields
and a gun
so tight.

Wild demon loneliness
crying the truth.
Madness is a plea,
to shine
in lost youth.

A drowning stillness,
his ear is gone.
Presented to
a young whore,
this coming dawn.

Journey

The spirit
that created me
also created
a creator with me.
My mediocrity has
brought forth the bearded,
the smoking,
thinking philosopher.
The artist that destiny
will forget,
the poet that
will die from drink,
the musician that
will astound the world,
and the teacher that
will show us the way.
I do not require praise,
just not disdain
for my being.
Do not gaze at me
as you do
the homeless man,
holding a sign,
asking for help.

Prey

Silent the moon's tongue
is slow and keen.
Unaware of danger,
the coat's eyes shine.
Certain death stares
and hum the dark.
A lunge, the force,
the strike, the fate.
Blood is untied,
a family eats.
Tomorrow's sun
will rise, and
the night repeats.

Fingerprint

It is very still.
The undertow moves
in broken guise.
Lingering in its
cruel comprehension,
it stretches long and slow.
It cannot vanish,
or pretend to amend,
the purpose for which
it lives. Sorrow
gets a mask,
the wound gets but
one stitch.
The fingerprint
of each day
lies with the
individual
fragile heart.

I Always Knew

I always thought
I knew who I was.
Yet, crowds and faces
sought to destroy me.
Their masks were loud,
covered in years
of dust. Playing roles
for which I laughed.
Their whispers are
strange, out of place.
I learned from
forgotten silences.
I unfolded into the
unknown, coming out
defined and flowing.

Vow of Dawn

Old seasons crawl
hand in hand, they
become undone.
To breathe again
together in laughter.
The vow of dawn
is shared, it is soft,
and it is true. Find
your breath beside you,
then make a home.

Loved That Boy

My father said,
"You know boy, Bob
sure loved old John.
Did you know they were
in the hospital together
when they died"?

"What"

"Yeah, Bob heard
that John had died,
walked down the hall
into his room, and
slapped him across
the face, then told
him to quit
fucking around."

"Jesus Christ"

"The problem was he
wasn't fucking around,
he was dead and
that destroyed Bob.
A couple of days later
he died too."

"I know Bob loved him,
but he was a piece of shit.
I had to punch
him once."

"I told you about
Bob asking me to
kick the shit out of

John didn't I?"

"No"

Bob finally had it with
him stealing money
from the bar, but he
loved that boy and
just couldn't do
it himself. So, he
paid me to do it."

"I assume you didn't
hurt him too bad."

"No, just a good old
fashion ass kicking.
But you know what,
that little fucker never
stole another dime
from Bob."

For Those Between Worlds

Stuck in shifting sand,
how to lift their feet
a gaze,
a sigh.
Unable, torn, searching
to feel, they are
pulled away.
Fractured, unsure the
path is undone,
then done again.
Home has always
been suspended,
for those
between worlds.

Bend Its Knee

He whispers,
the prophet's voice,
it is thunderously quiet.
In its grip the moon
will fall,
mountains will fly,
smoke will sink, and
the stars will run.
The stones will weep
with laughter
at the end. Nature
will bend its knee,
on the ashes
of the dead.

Sometimes When Someone Dies

When someone dies,
memories run rampant.
They are not always
fond memories
of your loved ones.
They are flashes of time,
sometimes unbearable.
I have seen
their faces for years,
but now I see
their existence.
They were evil in life,
and to me
they are evil in death.

Their age took them early,
because their soul was rotten,
course with disgust.
The reason for their lifelessness
rests with the hounds
that now guard their feet.

I do not blame my loved ones,
nor do I have any pity
for the family that
has lost so many souls.
These people, who were not
members of my family,
they stole from me

my childhood, the dreams,
and now my sleep.
I am glad
you are all dead.
I will not apologize,
and God
will understand.
I spit on you
and thank you
for being dead.
You saved me
time and effort.
I can sleep now
knowing you
are all in Hell.

I Have Seen My Moment

Before they go,
you might want to let them know
how unintended it may be,
they helped you become who you are.
The reason your children
are the beings they are
can be traced back to a single
point held in Gods hand.
That moment in which you
witnessed the birth of a thought
that became you.
You like sports
or playing an instrument
because at an early age
you looked the future in the eye.

For me it was eight years old,
I witnessed the coolest,
funniest, human
I had ever seen.
I watched as I grew older
how easy he made it
to raise a family
and get through each day.

In this world with drugs,
alcohol, and jail a normal
part of small-town life,
it was astonishing.

Great men should not
be considered great
because of how much money they have.
Bank accounts are nothing
compared to a good life
of day-to-day struggles.
We do not see these in most people,
these events are done
in silence, so it appears easy.
My children are who they are
because of who that man is.
He is who he is
because of that moment
in which he saw his future.
The only thing I know for sure,
that moment was as glorious
for him as it was for me.
I hope he still
remembers that moment,
and I hope his children
have seen their moment.
Mine have,
and I am grateful for that.

Odd Time to Become a Poet

Seventeen years old
is an odd time.
You think you know
what love is,
you think you are an adult.
You can drive a car;
it is expected that
you are having sex.
The physical pain
in the stomach is real.
But that does not make
you understand
the feelings behind it.
Something needed to get in there
and reach a part of you
that nothing else can.
Sometimes, a self-destructive force
invades in secret. Sometimes
it is hidden in
poetry books,
philosophy books,
or in movies.
Sometimes it can be in all
that surrounds you,
and you
are just doomed.
Hidden in the works
of Morrison, Nietzsche,
and Rimbaud

lies your future.
It contains both your
pain and redemption.
Your good days
and bad days,
the voices,
the alcohol, the drugs
you have not even done yet,
watch and wait.
They want your soul,
and they make bets
on whether they will get it
or not.
Sometimes it takes years
for the captures,
sometimes it takes
only months. Sometimes
they never get it,
and they get a
simple thank you instead.

Like Patti Smith

Like Patti Smith,
no one knew I was coming.
I was aware the grass
would not be green.
But I did not know
if the sagebrush would cry,
burn, or sing.
I was driving an old car
that was going to make it,
or it wasn't.
I had one cassette tape,
just enough gas money,
stolen registration tags,
and a single joint.

I slept in the car.
It was no big deal
since I had lived in my car
from time to time anyway.
I kept an alarm clock,
a sleeping bag,
and a pillow in it,
always.
I was leaving a life where
my only meal consisted of
a ninety-nine cent McDonald's meal
once a day.
Most of this
was my own doing.

My desire to get a college degree
consumed me. I needed to go
somewhere to get a job
and save money.
I was never the loser
people always thought I was,
and I needed to prove it.

When I arrived with five dollars
in my pocket
and a single bag of clothes,
I gave my car away.
What I was really doing
was giving away a memory
I no longer wanted.
They had never seen
a person like me.
Yet, after time
they took me as their own,
but I never fit in. I guess
I don't really fit in anywhere.
The years went by
with the sagebrush crying
my own song,
and burning due
to my own undoing.
But I made it sing
with desire. I got what
I came for.
I left destruction
along the way,
but I did it.

I tuned failure
into success,
and I loved
every second of it.

The Brain

The brain remembers
what it wants.
It changes,
it fools,
and it displays the world
sometimes not as it is.
Then again, sometimes
it shows us the world
exactly how it is.

It flashes the brilliance
of childhood
and skips a beat
on your present location.
It spills tears
when least appropriate
and expresses anger at a rose.
It smells the desperation
of a dog's heat,
then tosses aside
the goals completion.

It grows, changes,
and distorts one's age.
Clinging to its vibrant
muse of contentment.
It drives cars,
has babies,

and plunges
souls into peril.
What a great device
the brain is.

Indian Artifacts

I was not sure
what was going on,
but I knew something was.
My father and little sister
were still asleep,
and my mother was in the bathroom
with the door open
putting her make up on.
I was talking to her
as I did a lot,
my head up against the wall
in the hallway and my feet
on the other wall.
I do not remember
if she told me to get
my feet off the wall.
I am guessing she did not
since the circumstances
of this morning were different.
She was going out of town by herself
because my grandfather had died.
I did not really know the man very well,
but what I had heard
of him over the years
was never good.
I think the only time
I remembered anybody
saying good things
about him

was a story my father told me.
He said some guys
were out back in the alleyway
about to whoop his ass,
then out of nowhere
my grandfather
reached over the fence
with a .357 and
made it clear
nobody was getting
their ass whooped today.
At the time
I did not understand
why I could not go with her.
I went everywhere with my mom
when I was young.
But she was right in
making me stay.
As it turned out
the circumstances
of my grandfather's demise
were not ideal.
Much like the Indian skeleton
he dug up and kept for a souvenir,
he must have had
his own personal secrets,
and reasons for doing
what he did.
My guess would be
it was not a good site
when he took his own life.
I would also think
some people mourned his loss

or even felt some guilt,
others felt a sense of freedom.
I remember feeling nothing,
there was no real
attachment for me.
I am not sure the man
ever liked me.

Over the years
I have heard stories
about him,
nothing ever good.
I did hear that for a man
with very little education
he was able read and
understand the great works
of literature up to that time.
I know he liked to look
for Indian artifacts,
and collected
a huge quantity of them.
I got stoned one night
and attempted to put
those old Indian bones together
as they should be.
I scattered them out across
the living room floor and
turned the television on.
I never figured out
where everything went.
I also never figured out
why my grandfather
found the need to
commit suicide.

Studio Apartment

It started
with a simple phone call.
His friend wanted to stop
by when he came to town
and use the phone
in exchange for a little weed.
Obviously, he did not feel
it was safe
to use his own phone.
From the window
of his studio apartment,
he sees the car pull up.
It is the same
piece of shit Dodge.
Two guys step out of the car,
he recognizes the driver,
but he looks like shit.
He has never seen
the other guy.
They walk up the stairs
and knock on the door.
Once they know
they are in the right place
and the deal to use the phone
is all good,
they head back to the car.

Watching from the window
he can see his friend

grabbing a duffle bag
out of the trunk,
his companion pulls out
a sawed-off shotgun.
They both walk upstairs
and into the apartment.
His friend hands
him a bag of weed
and asks for the phone.
The other guy
opens the duffle bag
and puts its contents
on the coffee table.
There must have been
a hundred thousand dollars
worth of drugs sitting there
next to a stranger
with a sawed-off shotgun.
He did not know
if it was coke or meth,
but he knew
he had just fucked up.

Our Shadows

We were trees, roots
tangled together
for fifty years.
The growing weight
of life, mapped
our jokes. Our shadows
mocked each other.

Walking in song
we were sheltered
from the ghosts.
We laughed at storms
and dreamed of the moon,
that would hang forever,
over the old neighborhood.

Bowls

All I ever wanted
was a regular life.
To a kid
the meaning
of that would vary
depending on each kid.
For me,
that was cereal bowls.
Every time
I would spend the night
at a friend's house,
we had cereal
in matching bowls.
For some reason,
that little thing
stood out to me
as what normal
people have.
Their houses
were not different.
Their cars
were the same.
But their dishes
had a full set
of matching bowls.

Man with a Plan

He was hit
just above the left eye
with an ashtray.
I assume the guy
knew he could not
knock him out, so he used
the heavy ashtray
resting on the bar.
It knocked him down,
for about two seconds.
When he got back up,
he was pissed off,
and fully aware
of what had happened,
and who had done it.
His glasses were broken
into pieces and blood
was dripping from his face,
but this was not
going to be the end.
This man was supposed
to be his friend.

Like a coward the man
ran from the bar,
he knew if he was caught
it might be his last day
on earth. He crossed the street
and ran and hid

behind the bar
of another establishment.
That in and of itself
goes against all common decency
for those that frequent
those types of bars.
You could get hurt
doing something like that.
The patrons were good
in this situation. They knew
the crazed man,
they had seen him mad
many times.
They wanted to give up the man
hiding behind the bar, but feared
what would become of him.
That coward of a man
lived another day,
but he did get
what was coming to him.
The crazed man
when things settled down,
also became a man with a plan.

The Nest

The youngling's cradle
once rested high.
Soared beyond the moon,
danced in the sky.
It was to be taught
to fly without fear.
Now its future
seems unclear.
No shadow appears
to quench its thirst.
Dawn comes each day,
as its trembling gets worse.

Hearts are Ignored

The running touch
carved a beacon.
Voices all
spoke as one.
Hope and joy
were ballots, pondering
the future of promise.

Robes began to jingle,
coins fell to the ground.
Greed, bent to retrieve
and hearts are ignored.

The truth is drowned,
sold at auction. Toasts
were none, for hungry
hands had debt.
Rebel thoughts
became fierce.

Hold On

Running bright,
begging
whispered delight.
To love, be bold
and to hold
on
to the poison
until later.
Do not be cruel,
I am coming,
in time.

Let me kiss,
and dance
the petal,
those threads
forever. Bury
my heart
open,
reclaimed
and loved.

The Rose

You had the breath,
of lullabies.
Your promises
of perfume
were as sacred,
as a kiss.

Now a ghost
who has betrayed,
walks the garden,
you let slip away.
Numb, you have soured.
The bloom is no more.

Two Whores

They were old
haggard souls. Sex
was their only tool
to survive the night.
Two of them
shared one small room.
Only one would be in there
at a time, anyway.

There motel was behind
the bar my father
hung out at, where I
at eight years old
would hustle pool.

The beef jerky was good,
the soda had ice, and I
had seen the old ladies.
They came into the bar,
drank during the day, maybe
got a customer or two.
They thought I was cute.
My father called them names.

Some old man got a check,
And wanted to celebrate. He got
a room in the back, some beer
to go, then walked into the room.

The two ladies were behind him.
They discussed the price.

He couldn't perform
what was expected. But,
they wanted their money.
They insulted the old man,
beat him, poured beer
over his head. Then
cleaned out his wallet.

Knife in the Gas Tank

They never caught the girl.
They young lady who after
a night of drinking, stabbed
her boyfriend to death. The knife
was a big X on a treasure map.
A bloody handprint, near the gas tank
of my father's old Ford Pinto.
The ugliest fucking car
I had ever seen.

I was just there
to pick my father up. While
I am waiting for the cops
to get their statements,
my father ordered me a beer.
The bartender never questioned it,
he just put Old Style in front of me.
I wasn't old enough to drink.
I think he was more afraid
of my father, than the cops outside.

Some drunkard sitting next
to us at the bar began to talk
about how he hasn't seen that
much blood since Vietnam. My father
did the math in his head. Then, he told the
guy to shut the fuck up. There was
no way he was in Vietnam.

I finished my beer and me
and my father walked out the door.
As we walked to my car
I could see the blood
next to the gas tank. A cop said
he wanted to ask my father
some questions about what happened.
My father also told him
to fuck off.

www.ingramcontent.com/pod-product-compliance
Ingram Content Group UK Ltd.
Pitfield, Milton Keynes, MK11 3LW, UK
UKHW041315190726
13845UKWH00025B/290

9 789363 543713